THE OXFORD PIANO METHOD

PIANO TIME CARO

19 really easy arrangements by

Pauline Hall

T0087068

CONTENTS

Away in a manger	2
I saw three ships	3
Kings of Orient	4
In dulci jubilo	6
Good King Wenceslas	7
O come, all ye faithful	8
While shepherds watched their flocks	10
Deck the hall	11
The first Nowell	12
Silent night	14
Once in royal David's city	15
God rest you merry, gentlemen	16
In the bleak mid-winter	18
The holly and the ivy	19
A merry Christmas	20
Jingle, bells	22
Hark! the herald-angels sing	24
Ding dong! merrily on high	26
O little town of Bethlehem	28

This book belongs to _____

Address _____

Date _____

Away in a manger

W. J. Kirkpatrick (1838–1921)

1. A - way in a man - ger, no crib for a bed, The lit - tle Lord Je - sus laid down his sweet head; The stars in the bright sky looked down where he lay, The lit - tle Lord Je - sus a - sleep on the hay.

2 The cattle are lowing,
The baby awakes,
But little Lord Jesus
No crying he makes.
I love thee, Lord Jesus!
Look down from the sky,
And stay by my side until
Morning is nigh.

3 Be near me, Lord Jesus;
I ask thee to stay
Close by me for ever,
And love me, I pray.
Bless all the dear children
In thy tender care,
And fit us for heaven,
To live with thee there.

Anon.

© Oxford University Press 1994
Printed in Great Britain
OXFORD UNIVERSITY PRESS, MUSIC DEPARTMENT, GREAT CLARENDON STREET, OXFORD OX2 6DP
Photocopying this copyright material is ILLEGAL.

I saw three ships

English traditional carol

2 And what was in those ships all three?
On Christmas Day, on Christmas Day,
And what was in those ships all three?
On Christmas Day in the morning.

3 Our Saviour Christ and his Lady.

4 Pray, whither sailed those ships all three?

5 O, they sailed into Bethlehem.

6 And all the bells on earth shall ring.

Kings of Orient

Optional accompaniment

Kings of Orient

Words and melody by J. H. Hopkins (1820–91)

Solo*

We three kings of O - ri - ent are; Bear - ing gifts we

tra - verse a - far Field and foun - tain, moor and moun - tain,

Fol - low - ing yon - der star: O *star of won - der,*

star of night, Star with ro - yal beau - ty bright, West - ward

lead - ing, still pro - ceed - ing, Guide us to thy per - fect light.

*To be played 1 octave higher if accompaniment is used.

In dulci jubilo

German, 14th-century
tr. R. L. Pearsall (1795–1856)

Old German carol

In dul - ci ju - bi - lo[a] Let us our ho - mage

shew; Our heart's joy re - clin - eth *In prae -*

- se - pi - o[b] And like a bright star shin -

- eth *Ma - tris in gre - mi - o.*[c] *Al - pha*

es et O,[d] *Al - pha es et O!*

[a] in tuneful joy [b] in a stable [c] on his mother's lap [d] You are Alpha and Omega–the beginning and the end.

Good King Wenceslas

Melody from *Piae Cantiones* (1582)

2 'Hither, page, and stand by me,
If thou know'st it, telling,
Yonder peasant, who is he?
Where and what his dwelling?'
'Sire, he lives a good league hence,
Underneath the mountain,
Right against the forest fence,
By Saint Agnes' fountain.'

3 'Bring me flesh, and bring me wine,
Bring me pine-logs hither:
Thou and I will see him dine,
When we bear them thither.'
Page and monarch, forth they went,
Forth they went together;
Through the rude wind's wild lament
And the bitter weather.

4 'Sire, the night is darker now,
And the wind blows stronger;
Fails my heart, I know not how;
I can go no longer.'
'Mark my footsteps, good my page;
Tread thou in them boldly:
Thou shalt find the winter's rage
Freeze thy blood less coldly.'

5 In his master's steps he trod,
Where the snow lay dinted;
Heat was in the very sod
Which the saint had printed.
Therefore, Christian men, be sure,
Wealth or rank possessing,
Ye who now will bless the poor,
Shall yourselves find blessing.

J. M. Neale (1818–66)

O come, all ye faithful

Optional accompaniment

O come, all ye faithful

tr. F. Oakeley (1802–80) and others

Words and melody by J. F. Wade (*c.*1711-86)

Solo*

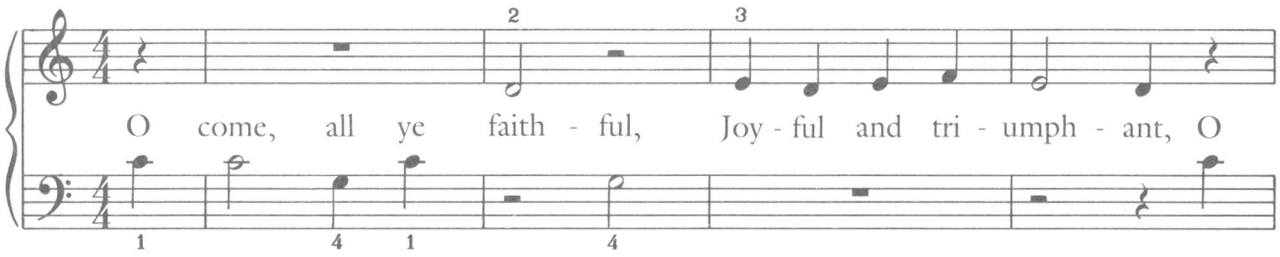

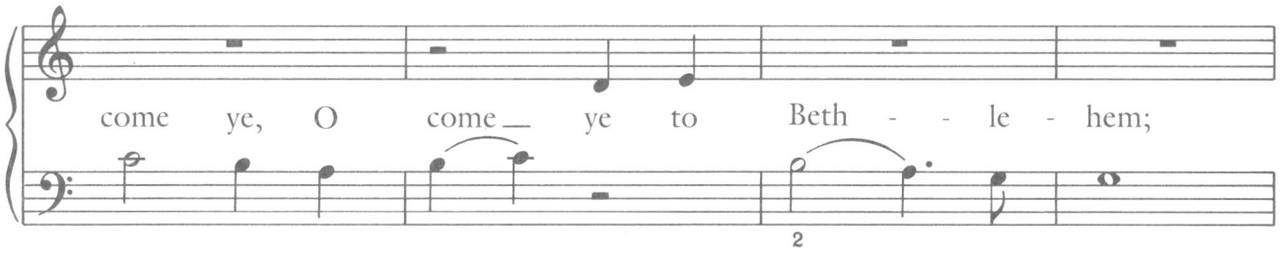

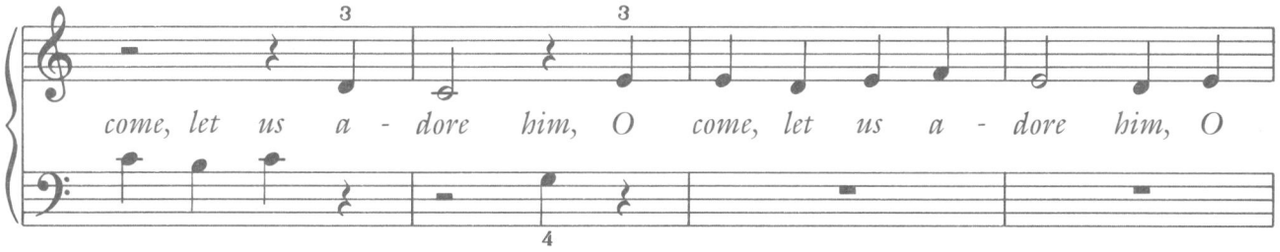

*To be played 1 octave higher if accompaniment is used.

While shepherds watched their flocks

'Winchester Old'

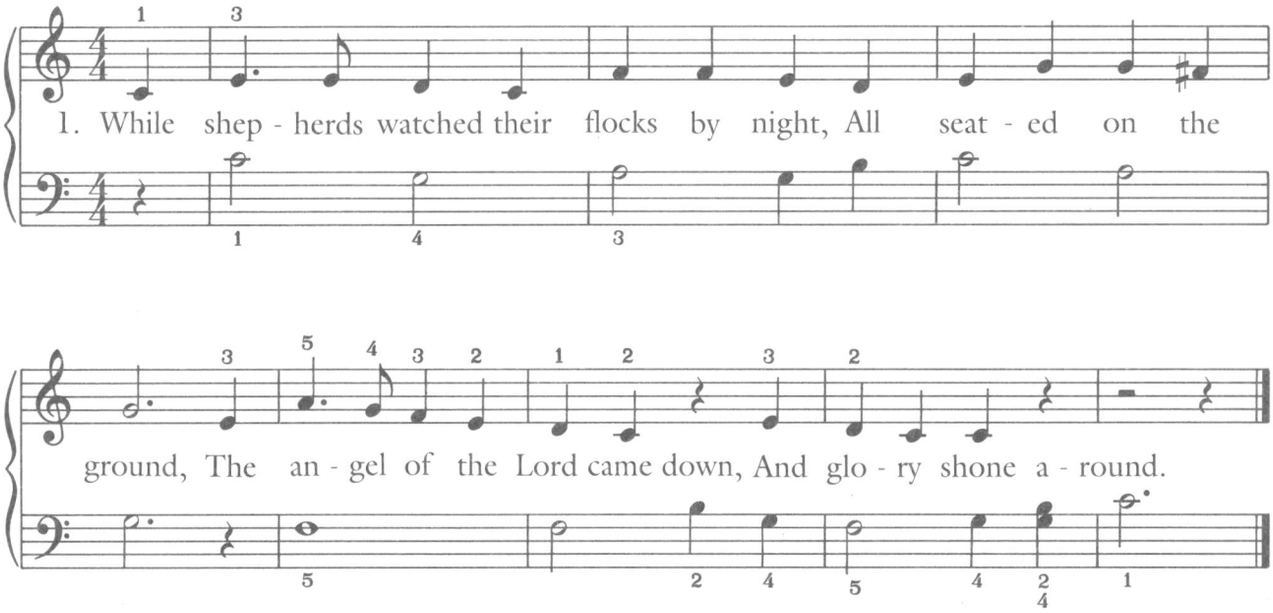

2 'Fear not,' said he (for mighty dread
Had seized their troubled mind);
'Glad tidings of great joy I bring
To you and all mankind.

3 'To you in David's town this day
Is born of David's line
A Saviour, who is Christ the Lord;
And this shall be the sign:

4 'The heav'nly Babe you there shall find
To human view displayed,
All meanly wrapped in swathing bands,
And in a manger laid.'

5 Thus spake the seraph; and forthwith
Appeared a shining throng
Of angels praising God, who thus
Addressed their joyful song:

6 'All glory be to God on high,
And to the earth be peace;
Goodwill henceforth from heav'n to men
Begin and never cease.'

N. Tate (1652–1715)

Deck the hall

Welsh traditional carol

Solo [Right hand only]

Deck the hall with boughs of hol - ly, *Fa la la la la, fa la la la,*

'Tis the sea - son to be jol - ly, *Fa la la la la, fa la la la.*

Fill the mead cup, drain the bar - rel, *Fa la la, fa la la, la la la,*

Troll the an - cient Christ - mas ca - rol, *Fa la la la la, fa la la la.*

Accompaniment

The first Nowell

Optional accompaniment

The first Nowell

English traditional carol

Solo*

The first No - well the an - gel did say Was to

cer - tain poor shep - herds in fields as they lay; In fields where

they lay, keep - ing their sheep, On a cold win - ter's night that

was so deep: *No - well, No - well, No - well, No -*

- well, Born is the King of Is - ra - el!

*To be played 1 octave higher if accompaniment is used.

Silent night

Franz Gruber (1787–1863)

1. Si - lent night, ho - ly night, All is calm,

all is bright; Round yon vir - gin mo - ther and child.

Ho - ly in - fant so ten - der and mild, Sleep in hea - ven - ly

peace, Sleep in hea - ven-ly peace.

2 Silent night, holy night,
Shepherds first saw the sight:
Glories stream from heaven afar,
Heav'nly hosts sing Alleluia:
Christ the Saviour is born,
Christ the Saviour is born!

J. Mohr (1792–1848)

Once in royal David's city

H. J. Gauntlett (1805–76)

Solo [with optional accompaniment]

1. Once in ro - yal Da - vid's_ ci - ty stood a low - ly cat - tle_ shed,
Where a mo - ther laid_ her_ ba - by in a man - ger for_ his_ bed:

Ma - ry was that mo - ther mild, Je - sus Christ her lit - tle_ child.

Optional accompaniment

R.H.
L.H.

2 He came down to earth from heaven,
Who is God and Lord of all,
And his shelter was a stable,
And his cradle was a stall;
With the poor, and mean, and lowly,
Lived on earth our Saviour holy.

3 And our eyes at last shall see him,
Through his own redeeming love,
For that child so dear and gentle
Is our Lord in heav'n above;
And he leads his children on
To the place where he is gone.

C. F. Alexander (1818–95)

God rest you merry, gentlemen

Optional accompaniment

2 From God our heav'nly Father
A blessed angel came,
And unto certain shepherds
Brought tidings of the same,
How that in Bethlehem was born
The Son of God by name:
O tidings of comfort and joy,
Comfort and joy,
O tidings of comfort and joy.

3 Now to the Lord sing praises,
All you within this place,
And with true love and brotherhood
Each other now embrace;
This holy tide of Christmas
All others doth deface:
O tidings of comfort and joy,
Comfort and joy,
O tidings of comfort and joy.

God rest you merry, gentlemen

English traditional carol

Solo*

1. God rest you mer - ry, gen - tle - men, let no - thing you dis - may, For

Je - sus Christ our Sa - viour was born up - on this day, To save us all from

Sa - tan's power when we were gone a - stray: *O___ ti - dings of com - fort and*

joy, com - fort and joy, O___ ti - dings of com - fort and joy.

*To be played 1 octave higher if accompaniment is used.

In the bleak mid-winter

Gustav Holst (1874–1934)

2 Our God, Heav'n cannot hold him
Nor earth sustain;
Heav'n and earth shall flee away
When he comes to reign:
In the bleak mid-winter
A stable-place sufficed
The Lord God Almighty
Jesus Christ.

3 What can I give him,
Poor as I am?
If I were a shepherd
I would bring a lamb,
If I were a Wise Man
I would do my part, —
Yet what I can I give him,
Give my heart.

C. Rossetti (1830–94)

The holly and the ivy

English traditional carol

1. The hol - ly and the i - vy when they are both full grown; Of all the trees that are in the wood the hol - ly bears the crown. *The ri - sing of the sun and the run - ning of the deer, The play - ing of the mer - ry or - gan, sweet sing - ing in the choir.*

2 The holly bears a blossom
As white as any flower;
And Mary bore sweet Jesus Christ
To be our sweet Saviour.
The rising of the sun (*etc.*)

3 The holly bears a prickle
As sharp as any thorn;
And Mary bore sweet Jesus Christ
On Christmas Day in the morn.
The rising of the sun (*etc.*)

A merry Christmas

Optional accompaniment

A merry Christmas

English traditional carol

Solo*

We wish you a mer-ry Christ-mas, We wish you a mer-ry Christ-mas, We

wish you a mer - ry Christ - mas And a hap - py New Year. *Good*

ti - dings we bring To you and your kin; We

wish you a mer - ry Christ - mas And a hap - py New Year.

*To be played 1 octave higher if accompaniment is used.

Jingle, bells

Optional accompaniment

Jingle, bells

Words and melody by J. Pierpont (1822–93)

Solo*

Dash-ing through the snow in a one - horse o - pen sleigh, O - ver fields we

go, laugh-ing all the way; Bells on Bob-tail ring, mak - ing spi - rits

bright; What fun it is to ride, and sing a sleigh - ing song to - night!

Jin - gle, bells, jin - gle, bells, Jin - gle all the way; Oh, what fun it

is to ride in a one - horse o - pen sleigh! Oh, one - horse o - pen sleigh!

*To be played 1 octave higher if accompaniment is used.

Hark! the herald-angels sing

Optional accompaniment

2 Christ, by highest heav'n adored,
Christ, the everlasting Lord,
Late in time behold him come,
Offspring of a virgin's womb!
Veiled in flesh the Godhead see,
Hail th'incarnate Deity,
Pleased as Man with man to dwell,
Jesus, our Emmanuel!
Hark! the herald-angels sing
Glory to the new-born King.

3 Hail the heav'n-born Prince of Peace!
Hail the Sun of Righteousness!
Light and life to all he brings,
Ris'n with healing in his wings;
Mild he lays his glory by,
Born that man no more may die,
Born to raise the sons of earth,
Born to give them second birth.
Hark! the herald-angels sing
Glory to the new-born King.

Charles Wesley (1707–88) and others

Hark! the herald-angels sing

F. Mendelssohn (1809–47)

Solo*

1. Hark! the he - rald - an - gels sing_ Glo - ry to the new-born King; Peace on earth and

mer - cy mild,_ God and sin - ners re - con - ciled: Joy - ful all ye na - tions rise,_

Join the tri - umph of the skies;_ With th'an - ge - lic host pro - claim, Christ is_born in

Beth - le - hem. *Hark! the he - rald an - gels sing Glo - ry_ to the new - born King.*

*To be played 1 octave higher if accompaniment is used.

Ding dong! merrily on high

16th-century French melody

Solo
1. Ding dong! mer - ri - ly on high in heav'n the bells are ring - ing:
Ding dong! ve - ri - ly the sky is riv'n with an - gels sing - ing.
Glo - - -

Ding Dong! merrily on high

Accompaniment

2 E'en so here below, below,
Let steeple bells be swungen,
And *i-o, i-o, i-o,*
By priest and people sungen.
Gloria! Hosanna in excelsis!

3 Pray you, dutifully prime
Your matin chime, ye ringers;
May you beautifully rime
Your evetime song, ye singers.
Gloria! Hosanna in excelsis!

G. R. Woodward (1848–1934)

O little town of Bethlehem

English traditional carol
coll. and arr. by R. Vaughan Williams

1. O lit - tle town of Beth - le - hem, how still we _ see thee lie! A -
- bove thy deep and dream - less _ sleep the si - lent _ stars go by. Yet _
in thy dark _ streets _ shin - eth the e - ver - last - ing light; The
hopes and fears of all _ the _ years are met in _ thee to - night.

2 O morning stars, together
Proclaim the holy birth,
And praises sing to God the King,
And peace to men on earth;
For Christ is born of Mary;
And, gathered all above,
While mortals sleep, the angels keep
Their watch of wondering love.

P. Brooks (1835–93)

© Oxford University Press. Adapted by permission.

Reproduced and printed by Halstan & Co. Ltd., Amersham, Bucks., England